Apress Pocket Guides

Apress Pocket Guides present concise summaries of cutting-edge developments and working practices throughout the tech industry. Shorter in length, books in this series aims to deliver quick-to-read guides that are easy to absorb, perfect for the time-poor professional.

This series covers the full spectrum of topics relevant to the modern industry, from security, AI, machine learning, cloud computing, web development, product design, to programming techniques and business topics too.

Typical topics might include:

- A concise guide to a particular topic, method, function or framework

- Professional best practices and industry trends

- A snapshot of a hot or emerging topic

- Industry case studies

- Concise presentations of core concepts suited for students and those interested in entering the tech industry

- Short reference guides outlining 'need-to-know' concepts and practices.

More information about this series at https://link.springer.com/ bookseries/17385.

Virtual Threads, Structured Concurrency, and Scoped Values

Explore Java's New Threading Model

Ron Veen
David Vlijmincx

Apress®

Virtual Threads, Structured Concurrency, and Scoped Values: Explore Java's New Threading Model

Ron Veen
ENSCHEDE, The Netherlands

David Vlijmincx
HELMOND, The Netherlands

ISBN-13 (pbk): 979-8-8688-0499-1
https://doi.org/10.1007/979-8-8688-0500-4

ISBN-13 (electronic): 979-8-8688-0500-4

Managing Director, Apress Media LLC: Welmoed Spahr
Acquisitions Editor: Melissa Duffy
Development Editor: Laura Berendson
Coordinating Editor: Gryffin Winkler

Cover designed by eStudioCalamar

Distributed to the book trade worldwide by Apress Media, LLC, 1 New York Plaza, New York, NY 10004, U.S.A. Phone 1-800-SPRINGER, fax (201) 348-4505, e-mail orders-ny@springer-sbm.com, or visit www.springeronline.com. Apress Media, LLC is a California LLC and the sole member (owner) is Springer Science + Business Media Finance Inc (SSBM Finance Inc). SSBM Finance Inc is a **Delaware** corporation.

For information on translations, please e-mail booktranslations@springernature.com; for reprint, paperback, or audio rights, please e-mail bookpermissions@springernature.com.

Apress titles may be purchased in bulk for academic, corporate, or promotional use. eBook versions and licenses are also available for most titles. For more information, reference our Print and eBook Bulk Sales web page at http://www.apress.com/bulk-sales.

Any source code or other supplementary material referenced by the author in this book is available to readers on GitHub (https://github.com/Apress). For more detailed information, please visit https://www.apress.com/gp/services/source-code.

If disposing of this product, please recycle the paper

Table of Contents

About the Authors...ix

About the Technical Reviewer xi

Introduction xiii

Chapter 1: Virtual Threads...1

Existing Threading Model..1

    Using Threads...2

    Using the Executor Service 4

    Async Programming 6

Virtual Threads...9

    Carrier Threads...16

    Mounting and Unmounting 18

    Pinned Virtual Threads...19

    When Not to Use Virtual Threads 22

Summary...24

Chapter 2: Structured Concurrency 27

What Is Structured Concurrency? 27

    Unstructured Concurrency..28

    Structured Concurrency..29

StructuredTaskScope 29

    Basic Example of StructuredTaskScope 30

    Subtasks...32

Using Virtual Threads by Default...34

Handling Timeouts...35

Structured ConcurrencyPolicies 35

Implementing Our Own Strategy 40

Structured Concurrency Alternatives 43

Completable Futures 43

Reactive Programming...44

Summary..46

Chapter 3: Scoped Values 47

What Are ThreadLocal Variables Again?..47

How ThreadLocals Work 48

How ThreadLocals Work Internally 50

Advantages of ThreadLocals...51

Disadvantages of ThreadLocals...52

Introducing Scoped Values..54

A Simple ScopedValue Example 55

Supplying More Than One ScopedValue.....................................57

When No Value Is Bound...57

Summing Up Scoped Values..59

Scope Binding Revisited..60

Final Thoughts 63

Summary..64

Chapter 4: Concurrency Patterns...**65**

How to Reason About Virtual Threads 65

How to Use Virtual Threads in Your Application....................................66

　　Virtual Threads for Web Applications 71

　　Using CompletableFuture<T> with Virtual Threads........................74

Summary..75

Index...**77**

About the Authors

Ron Veen is an experienced software engineer who has seen it all, from mainframes to microservices. Through all of this, he is guided by his passion for software engineering and software architecture.

For more than 15 years, he has been working on the JVM and the Java ecosystem and has seen all the frameworks and libraries from Apache to ZK.

Ron is an Oracle Certified Java Programmer (OCP) and Sun Certified Business Component Developer (SCBCD/OCPBCD).

He is an international speaker at software conferences and has published several books on Java and Jakarta EE.

David Vlijmincx is a developer with 8+ years of experience, Oracle ACE, author, blogger, and conference speaker with a passion for Java development. He has been working in the industry since 2016 and has a deep understanding of Java and its capabilities. He is always looking for new and innovative ways to solve complex problems and strives to stay up to date with the latest technologies and best practices in the field. Currently, he is working as a software consultant.

About the Technical Reviewer

Manuel Jordan Elera is an autodidactic developer and researcher who enjoys learning new technologies for his own experiments and creating new integrations. Manuel won the Springy Award 2013 Community Champion and Spring Champion. In his little free time, he reads the Bible and composes music on his guitar. Manuel is known as dr_pompeii. He has tech-reviewed numerous books, including *Pro Spring MVC with WebFlux* (Apress, 2020), *Pro Spring Boot 2* (Apress, 2019), *Rapid Java Persistence and Microservices* (Apress, 2019), *Java Language Features* (Apress, 2018), *Spring Boot 2 Recipes* (Apress, 2018), and *Java APIs, Extensions and Libraries* (Apress, 2018). You can read his detailed tutorials on Spring Technologies and contact him through his blog at www.manueljordanelera.blogspot.com. You can follow Manuel on his Twitter account, @dr_pompeii.

Introduction

This book provides you with an introduction to the new features Project Loom adds to the Java language. Project Loom adds virtual threads, structured concurrency, and scoped values which help you as a developer to write better concurrent applications. Each of the chapters gives you an introduction to the topic and shows you when you should consider it or totally avoid it.

Chapter 1: The first chapter covers what virtual threads are and how they are different from the threads that we already had in previous Java versions. This will show the life cycle virtual threads go through while executing code and how it works or doesn't work in some situations.

Chapter 2: This chapter covers structured concurrency which is a totally new concept that has been added to the Java language. You will learn new ways of managing the lifetime of your threads and how to make relationships between threads more explicit.

Chapter 3: The third chapter covers a new and immutable way of sharing values between threads. With previous versions of Java, you could use thread local variables, but with Java 21 there is a new way that is better fitted to use with virtual threads. You will learn how these scoped values work and how they work with structured concurrency.

Chapter 4: In the final chapter, we go over how to reason about virtual threads, so you know how to best apply them and how to use them with common patterns. You will also learn how to start using virtual threads inside your Spring or Quarkus applications.

CHAPTER 1

Virtual Threads

Virtual threads are one of the biggest new features of Java 21 since Lambdas. They have a big impact on how we implement concurrent code. As you probably know, you can have millions of them at the same time, something that wasn't possible before with the virtual threads we had since Java 1.0. Before we dive deeper into what virtual threads are, it is good to know how threads we currently use work and what their limitations are.

To follow along with the examples in this chapter, you need to have Java 21 and an IDE of your liking.

Existing Threading Model

With Java 21, we get a new kind of thread, virtual threads. To understand why these new kinds of threads are groundbreaking and to understand the benefits of these threads, we need to understand how the threads before Java 21 worked. The old threads haven't gone anywhere; we can still use them; it's just that with Java 21, we get an extra kind of thread.

Creating a thread is straightforward. There is a big chance you have done something like the following to create a thread in a school, hobby, or work project:

© Ron Veen and David Vlijmincx 2024
R. Veen and D. Vlijmincx, *Virtual Threads, Structured Concurrency, and Scoped Values,*
Apress Pocket Guides, https://doi.org/10.1007/979-8-8688-0500-4_1

```
Runnable task = () -> System.out.println("Hello, Reader!");

Thread thread = new Thread(task);
thread.start();
```

The previous example shows a pretty easy way to create a thread. There are some interesting things that happen behind the scenes when you run this code. When you call the thread constructor, Java will go to the operating system (OS) and ask it to create an OS thread, because a thread in Java is just a very thin wrapper around a system thread. Each time you call the thread constructor, the application will ask the operating system to create a thread, which doesn't sound too bad, but to create such a thread is an expensive operation. The application needs to call the OS, and the OS in turn needs to create the system resource and allocate some memory that the thread can use.

The allocation of memory is different for each OS, but this can be 1 megabyte for each thread you create. This is the default for some systems. One megabyte doesn't sound too bad in an age where most laptops have 16GB RAM and servers can have terabytes of RAM, but it still creates a limit for the number of threads you can have. So why not allocate less memory by default? The problem is that the application doesn't know what you will do with the created thread. Is it going to use a little or much memory, it doesn't know when the thread is created. The memory of a thread lives off the heap, which means that the Java virtual machine (JVM) can resize it. Once it is created, it can't be resized.

Using Threads

You can use threads in a lot of ways, but let's go over some of the most popular ways of using threads and see what the benefits of these different approaches are.

The easiest way of using threads is by creating them for each task that you have. A task is defined as a single unit of work. So, the easiest way is to create a thread for each task that we have and discard it when it is done. To make it more visible in the following example, three tasks are created, and each task gets its own thread to run in:

```
Runnable task1 = () -> System.out.println("This is task 1!");
Runnable task2 = () -> System.out.println("This is task 2!");
Runnable task3 = () -> System.out.println("This is task 3");

Thread thread1 = new Thread(task1);
Thread thread2 = new Thread(task2);
Thread thread3 = new Thread(task3);

thread1.start();
thread2.start();
thread3.start();
```

In the previous example, a thread is created for each task. Three tasks run in their own thread, and when the task is done, the thread is discarded and cleaned up by the garbage collector. This is quite a wasteful way of programming because every time a thread is created, the application must create an OS thread and allocate some memory only to discard it when the task is done. While this is a very easy way of programming concurrent code, it doesn't make the best use of the system resources that are available.

Because we now have a virtual thread, we call these existing threads platform threads. They are called platform threads because they are managed by the platform instead of the application like virtual threads are.

Using the Executor Service

The previous examples were not very efficient. So, with Java 5, it is encouraged to use the executor services instead of the thread class directly. The executor service creates a pool of threads that you can submit tasks to. The benefit of this approach is that you don't have to manage the reusing of threads yourself, but Java will do this for you. This way, the threads are only created once and will be reused if the executor service is in scope. Let's take the previous example and try to improve it by using an executor instead of creating three threads ourselves.

Notice that in the example, the ExecutorService is created inside a try-with-resource statement. Starting with Java 21, the ExecutorService now implements the AutoCloseable interface. This means that it now implements the close method, and to exit the try-with-resource statement, all threads need to be finished either successfully or unsuccessfully.

```
Runnable task1 = () -> System.out.println("This is task 1!");
Runnable task2 = () -> System.out.println("This is task 2!");
Runnable task3 = () -> System.out.println("This is task 3!");

try(ExecutorService vte = Executors.newFixedThreadPool(3)){
    vte.submit(task1);
    vte.submit(task2);
    vte.submit(task3);
}
```

In the previous example, you can see the same three tasks as we had before, instead of creating a new thread for each task. We now submit them to an ExecutorService. What happens is that when a thread is available, it isn't executing another task; it will pick up a task from the queue. This is great! Now we can submit all the tasks we have, and we don't have to manage all these threads ourselves. But we can't have our cake and eat it too. There are also some downsides with the ExecutorService.

The first downside is that when a thread is blocked, it won't pick up a next task to run in the meantime. Threads rather block and wait than picking up a new task. This is problematic because we can only have a limited number of threads. These threads take up a relatively small amount of memory, but there is still a hard limit based on the amount of memory available. If you have a lot of small tasks, the changes are that you will be out of memory way before your CPU is fully utilized.

The next problem with ExecutorService is that threads are reused. You are probably wondering right now how this can be a good and a bad thing. Reusing threads is good, but there are little bugs that can sneak into your code when you are not careful with reusing threads. One of these problematic use cases is when tasks use thread local variables. When a task sets a thread local variable but forgets to unset it, the thread the task just ran on will be placed back into the pool with that thread local variable. The next task running on this thread will be able to read the thread local variable from the previous task. This is bad because then your thread local variables are leaking into other threads which can cause all kinds of trouble. Let's explore this problem in the following example:

```java
import java.util.concurrent.ExecutorService;
import java.util.concurrent.Executors;

public class Main {

    public static ThreadLocal<String> threadLocal = new
    ThreadLocal<>();

    public static void main(String[] args) {

        try (ExecutorService executor = Executors.
        newFixedThreadPool(1)) {

            executor.submit(() -> {
                threadLocal.set("Task 1 value");
```

```
                System.out.println("Task 1: " +
                threadLocal.get());
            });

            executor.submit(() -> {
                String value = threadLocal.get();
                System.out.println("Task 2: " + value);
            });
        }

    }

}
```

The output of the previous code example is as follows:

```
Task 1: Task 1 value
Task 2: Task 1 value
```

In the previous code example, we created two tasks and an executor service that uses a single thread to run these tasks. The first task sets a thread local variable but does not unset it. So, when task two runs on that same thread, it can access the thread local variable from task one which ran first on that thread. You can see this happening in the output where the value for tasks one and two is the same.

To summarize, the executor helps us to make better use of the system resources that are available to us while also giving us an easy way to have tasks run concurrently. Still, there are some downsides like the number of threads we can create and leaking of thread local variables.

Async Programming

We looked at how using the thread class is easy but not very efficient and how the ExecutorService makes reusing threads easier but still has some limitations. The next step is to look at async programming.

This is a relatively new programming model that makes better use of the system resources that are available to you. Let's look at some async code in action. In the following example, I use Vertx to create a server that listens on port 8080. When you run the following code, you can access the server from any browser using this URL: http://localhost:8080/.

```java
import io.vertx.core.Vertx;
public class Main {

    public static void main(String[] args) {
        Vertx.vertx().createHttpServer().requestHandler(req ->
        req.response().end("Hello from async code!"))
                .listen(8080, server -> {
            if (server.succeeded()) {
                System.out.println("Server started on
                port 8080");
            } else {
                System.err.println(server.cause());
            }
        });
    }

}
```

When running the previous example, you should see the following code in the console:

```
Server started on port 8080
```

This example clearly shows what it is doing and what happens when the creation of the server fails or succeeds. While this example is easy to follow, it can become confusing quite quickly, resulting in what is called the callback hell. Look at the following example to see what happens when we keep nesting async code within async code. The goal of the following code is to create a user and, if that action is successful, create an order and place it. The steps are broken up in multiple events that can either fail or succeed.

```java
public class Main {

    public static void main(String[] args) {
        Vertx.vertx().executeBlocking(event -> {
            try{
                User user = new User(1, "David");
                event.complete();
            }
            catch (Exception e){
                event.fail(e);
            }
        }, result -> {
            if(result.succeeded()){
                User david = (User )result.result();
                Order order = new Order(1, List.
                of("Milk","Cheese","Eggs"));

                Vertx.vertx().executeBlocking(event -> {
                    try{
                        // place the order
                        event.complete();
                    }
                    catch (Exception e){
                        event.fail(e);
                    }
                }, otherResult ->{
                    if (otherResult.succeeded()){
```

```
                        // continue
                    }
                });

            }
        });
    }

}
```

```
record User(int id,String name){}
record Order(int id, List<String> items){}
```

Like mentioned earlier, this code is not very readable or maintainable. So why would you want to use it? It does make very good use of the system resources that are available. When implementing your code like this, you don't have to worry about the maximum number of threads. Your CPU will be fully utilized before you run out of RAM because of thread memory.

While it makes better use of the system resources that are available, it is, in my opinion, the code that is hard to write and even harder to read, especially two weeks after you wrote it. Debugging code is also more difficult because Java and the JVM are built around stack frames, and that is something you lose when using asynchronous programming.

By now, you understand why and how concurrent code is written before Java 21 and what the upsides and downsides are of each approach. So let's take a look at the new kind of threads Java 21 has to offer!

Virtual Threads

Virtual threads are a new alternative implementation of the thread class. Don't worry, the existing thread we are familiar with is not going anywhere. With Java 21, we get a new kind of thread that still runs code as a single unit of work but is more lightweight.

Like I said, virtual threads are an alternative implementation, and the great thing about them is that the operating system doesn't know anything about them. Virtual threads are just a concept that lives inside your application. When you create virtual threads, there is no call made to the operating system, and no megabyte of system memory is allocated for it. Because virtual threads are just a simple instance of a class, they can simply store their stack frames on the heap, which has the great benefit of making the memory resizable! Creating a single virtual thread only takes a few bytes. When the virtual thread needs more memory, it can just allocate it. So, the stack of virtual threads is resizable. When it needs more memory, it can take it, and when it uses less, it is given back to the application.

So how cheap are these virtual threads? Let's check the memory usage by running two applications that are identical, but one uses platform threads and the other uses virtual threads. The goal of the application is to create a number of threads. Each thread was given the same task, to sleep for a given time. To get the memory usage, I used native memory tracking. The code of the application is as follows:

```
import java.time.Duration;
import java.util.concurrent.Executors;

public class Main {
    public static void main(String[] args) {
        long pid = ProcessHandle.current().pid();
        System.out.println("My PID is " + pid);

        // try(var exc = Executors.
        newVirtualThreadPerTaskExecutor()){
        try(var exc = Executors.
        newThreadPerTaskExecutor(Thread.ofPlatform().
        factory())){
            for (int i = 0; i < 1000; i++) {
```

```
            exc.submit(Main::sneakySleep);
        }
    }
}

private static void sneakySleep(){
    try {
        Thread.sleep(Duration.ofMinutes(2));
    } catch (InterruptedException e) {
        throw new RuntimeException(e);
    }
}
}
```

Inside the main method, a number of threads are created with the task to sleep for two minutes. While this is not something you would do in production code, it does show how much memory is needed to create that many instances of threads. Switching from one type of thread to another is simply done by commenting out a line. To see the memory usage, you need to pass the -XX:NativeMemoryTracking=detail as a VM option. You can add those inside the run configuration of your IDE.

In Figure 1-1, you can see the findings.

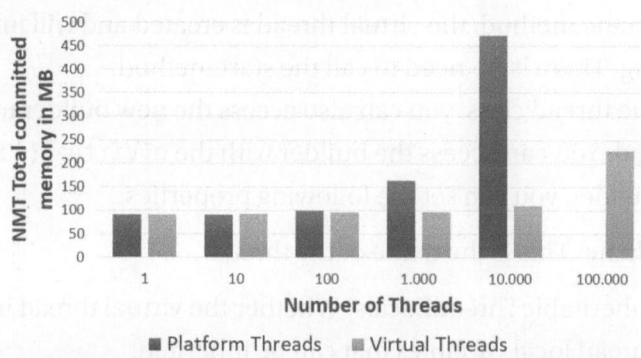

Figure 1-1. *Total memory usage of Virtual and Platform threads*

The result may surprise you, especially if you look at the first three runs of the application. There almost seems to be no difference when you either run 1, 10, or even 100 threads of any kind. Only when the applications created 100 threads, the version using platform threads uses a bit more memory. This tells us that if you already have an application that uses threads and less than 100 of them, it is not really worth it to rewrite the codebase, at least not for the small change in memory usage. But looking at 1000, 10,000, and 100,000 threads, the gap between virtual and platform threads starts to widen. At 100,000, the application using platform threads threw an out of memory exception. This shows that you can have a lot more virtual threads than platform threads.

Creating a virtual thread using the thread class is very straightforward. With Java 21, the thread class got a new static builder you can use to create a single virtual thread.

```
Runnable task = () -> System.out.println("Hello, World!");

Thread.startVirtualThread(task);
```

This is all you need to create a single thread. The first line creates a runnable that is going to run on the virtual thread. On the second line, the virtual thread is created. The static startVirtualThread method of the thread class is used. The method takes a runnable as a parameter. After calling the static method, the virtual thread is created and will immediately start running. There is no need to call the start method.

Using the thread class, you can also access the new builder to create a virtual thread. You can access the builder with the ofVirtual() method. Using the builder, you can set the following properties:

- Name: This is the name of the thread.

- InheritableThreadLocals: Whether the virtual thread inherits the thread local variables that can be inherited.

- uncaughtExceptionHandler: An exception handler for uncaught exceptions.

In the following example, you can see how to set the name of a virtual thread using the builder method:

```
Runnable task = () -> System.out.println("Hello, World!");

Thread.ofVirtual().name("vt1").start(task);

// not started
Thread unstarted = Thread.ofVirtual().name("vt 2").
unstarted(task);
unstarted.start();
```

The first builder creates a virtual thread with the name "vt 1" and gives the thread a task that will run after the method is called, while the second builder that creates virtual thread "vt 2" creates a thread that had not been started. To start the second virtual thread, you need to call start explicitly.

With the virtual thread builder, you can also create a factory. This factory can create virtual threads with the properties you set, for example, the name. This factory can be used with the existing executor services, so they use virtual threads instead of platform threads. In the following example, we create a virtual thread factory and use it with the newScheduledThreadPool:

```
ThreadFactory factory = Thread.ofVirtual().factory();
ScheduledExecutorService scheduledExecutorService = Executors.
newScheduledThreadPool(0, factory);

Callable<String> scheduledCallable = () -> {
    System.out.println("Done");
    return "Done";
};

scheduledExecutorService.schedule(scheduledCallable, 1,
TimeUnit.SECONDS);
```

In the preceding example, on the first line the virtual thread factory is created and is passed as a parameter to the newScheduledThreadPool. The pool will now create a virtual thread when a task is submitted to the pool.

With Java 21, we also get an executor service that uses virtual threads by default. The Executors.newVirtualThreadPerTaskExecutor() creates a virtual thread for each task that is submitted. It doesn't create a pool or anything like that. For each task, a new virtual thread is created. The thread will be discarded when the task is done. Threads are not reused, because they are really cheap to create. In the following example, you can see how to create the new executor:

```
Runnable task = () -> System.out.println("Hello, World!");

try(ExecutorService vte = Executors.
newVirtualThreadPerTaskExecutor()){
    vte.submit(task);
}
```

In the example, a newVirtualThreadPerTaskExecutor is created inside a try-with-resource statement, and a single task is submitted. The executor behaves the same as the other executors. The only difference is that this executor creates a new thread for each task. With this new executor, it is very easy to create a lot of threads by placing them in a for loop like this:

```
Runnable task = () -> System.out.println("Hello, World!");
try(ExecutorService vte = Executors.
newVirtualThreadPerTaskExecutor()){
    for (int i = 0; i < 1_000_000; i++) {
        vte.submit(task);
    }
}
```

In the previous example, a million tasks are submitted to the executor. This will result in a million virtual threads that get created. But how do these threads run on an actual system? Because we created an example with a lot more threads than cores in a system.

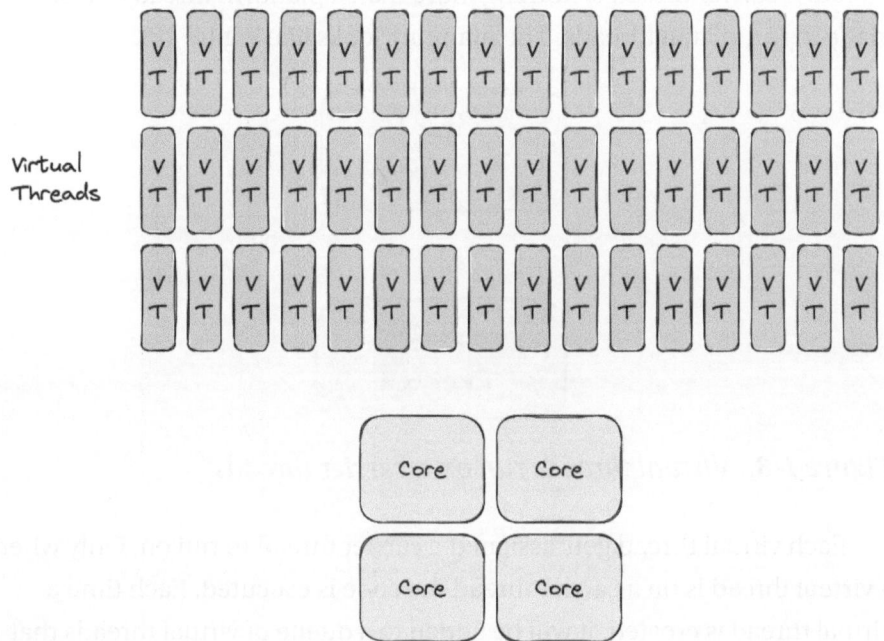

Figure 1-2. *How virtual threads get time to execute code*

In the previous code example, we created a million threads. To make this more visible, take a look at Figure 1-2 where we created more of virtual threads than there are cores available. Each of these virtual threads needs some time on the CPU core to actually run their task. The number of virtual threads can greatly outnumber the number of cores. In the next section, let's see how the system resources are shared between all those virtual threads.

Carrier Threads

A virtual thread does not directly run a thread that is managed by the operating system (platform thread). It runs on what is called a carrier thread. A carrier thread is nothing more than a platform thread that is made to run virtual threads. The mapping looks like Figure 1-3.

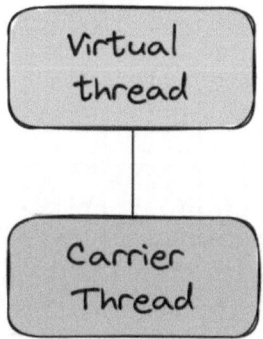

Figure 1-3. *Virtual threads run on a carrier threads*

Each virtual thread gets assigned a carrier thread to run on. Only when a virtual thread is on a carrier thread the code is executed. Each time a virtual thread is created, it will be added to a queue of virtual threads that will eventually be placed on a carrier thread. Let's add the queue and OS threads to the previous image to get a more complete picture of what happens.

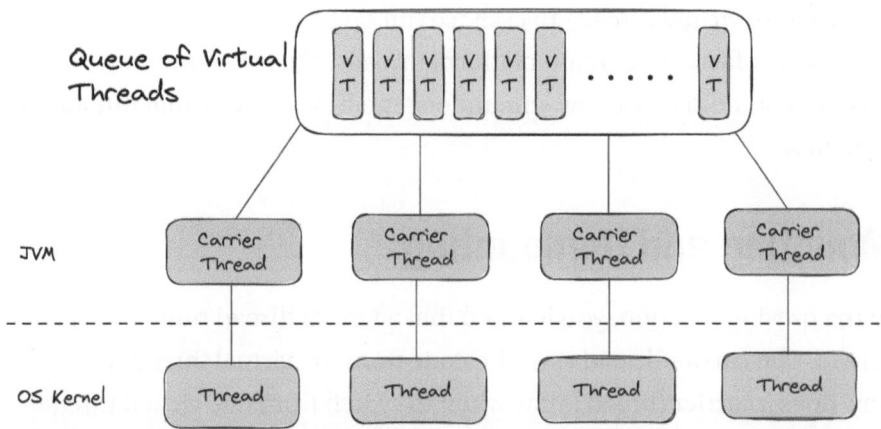

Figure 1-4. *Virtual threads are stored in a queue till they can run*

In Figure 1-4, you can see the virtual threads in their queue. They are assigned to a carrier thread in a first in, first out (FIFO) order. The carrier threads are from a dedicated forkjoinpool. These carrier threads are just platform threads which in turn are thin wrappers around system threads.

By default, you get as many carrier threads as there are cores inside your system. If you have a four-core system, you will get four carrier threads. There are ways to change the number of carrier threads you start with. Using the following property, you can change the number of carrier threads you have available:

```
jdk.virtualThreadScheduler.parallelism=5
```

The property can be used as a system property, or you can pass it as a VM option when running your application. With this parallelism value, the application would have five carrier threads. This can be useful if you want to reserve cores for other processes. You can also set it to a higher number than you have cores available, but carrier threads would have to share cores more often. This could cause a degradation in performance. So please make sure to measure the performance of your application.

Because virtual threads in essence run on platform threads, they can't be any faster than plain platform threads. This is a common misunderstanding, but now you understand how these virtual threads get their task done.

Mounting and Unmounting

In the previous section, you learned that a virtual thread runs on a carrier thread. The carrier thread runs the code from the virtual thread. But how does a carrier thread know when to switch from one virtual thread to another? A virtual thread will keep running on a carrier thread till it encounters a blocking method. If there is no blocking method, the virtual thread stays on the carrier thread, and you basically have a platform thread with the overhead of virtual threads.

The mechanism of moving a virtual thread on and off a carrier thread is called mounting and unmounting. When a virtual thread encounters a blocking method like a call to a database, it will get unmounted. This makes a place for a new virtual thread. The stack frames of the old virtual thread get copied from the carrier thread's memory into the heap. The stack frames of the new virtual thread will be copied from the heap into the carrier thread. This is one of the great features of virtual threads. The mounting and unmounting process makes sure that the carrier thread, which is an expensive resource, is always doing a task. The carrier thread is no longer blocked and doing nothing. Now it is running a new virtual thread, while the virtual thread that is blocked is now waiting to be unblocked in the heap. Virtual threads are very good at waiting. When the virtual thread is unblocked, it will be in the queue waiting to be picked up again. Figure 1-5 shows the complete cycle of this process.

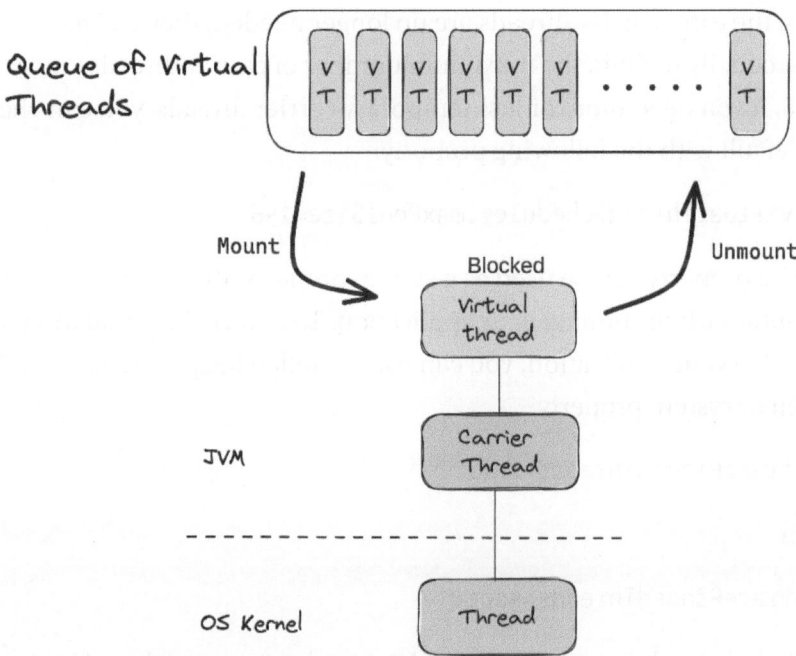

Figure 1-5. *Life cycle of virtual threads*

Pinned Virtual Threads

Some features of Java are not compatible with virtual threads yet. If the virtual thread enters a synchronized block, calls object.wait(), or makes a call to the native code using something like the Java Native Interface (JNI), unmounting a virtual thread does not happen. The virtual threads will then be stuck to the carrier threads. This causes that not only the virtual thread but also the carrier thread is blocked. When this happens, we say that the virtual thread is pinned to the carrier thread. If this happens for a short amount of time, it's fine, but if virtual threads are pinned to the carrier thread, this causes a degradation in performance.

To prevent a performance degradation, the JVM will help you by creating temporary extra carrier threads. These carrier threads will get new virtual threads to run while the existing carrier thread is blocked.

When the extra carrier threads are no longer needed, they will be discarded. By default, the maximum number of carrier threads you can get is 256. If you need more or less temporary carrier threads, you can change the default with the following property:

```
jdk.virtualThreadScheduler.maxPoolSize=256
```

The property can be used as a system property, or you can pass it as a VM option when running your application. To detect if a virtual thread is pinned in your application, you can use the following properties as a VM option or system property:

```
jdk.tracePinnedThreads=full
```

or

```
jdk.tracePinnedThreads=short
```

Both these options cause the JVM to log when a virtual thread is pinned. But the amount of information differs between them. With the short description, you see something like this when a virtual thread is pinned. To see the difference, try running the following example with the two values. The code creates three virtual threads that all call the same synchronized method:

```
public class DemoPinnedThread  {

    public static void main(String[] args) throws
    InterruptedException {

        Main main = new Main();

        Thread thread = Thread.startVirtualThread(() ->
        DemoPinnedThread.causesPinning(0));
        Thread thread1 =Thread.startVirtualThread(() ->
        DemoPinnedThread.causesPinning(1));
        Thread thread2 =Thread.startVirtualThread(() ->
        DemoPinnedThread.causesPinning(2));
```

```
    thread.join();
    thread1.join();
    thread2.join();

}

static synchronized public void causesPinning(int i) {

    System.out.println("i = " + i);
    try {
        Thread.sleep(1000);
    } catch (InterruptedException e) {
        throw new RuntimeException(e);
    }
}
}
```

This code has a method called causesPinning that causes the virtual threads to be pinned. With the full description, you will get the following output for each thread:

```
i = 0
Thread[#31,ForkJoinPool-1-worker-1,5,CarrierThreads]
    java.base/java.lang.VirtualThread$VThreadContinuation.
    onPinned(VirtualThread.java:185)
    java.base/jdk.internal.vm.Continuation.
    onPinned0(Continuation.java:393)
    java.base/java.lang.VirtualThread.parkNanos(VirtualThread.
    java:631)
    java.base/java.lang.VirtualThread.sleepNanos(VirtualThread.
    java:803)
    java.base/java.lang.Thread.sleep(Thread.java:507)
    org.example.DemoPinnedThread.
    causesPinning(DemoPinnedThread.java:24) <== monitors:1
```

```
org.example.DemoPinnedThread.lambda$main$0
(DemoPinnedThread.java:10)
java.base/java.lang.VirtualThread.run(VirtualThread.
java:311)
```

From the output, you can see that the pinning message is thrown when the thread enters the sleep method in the synchronized block. The short description looks like the following:

```
i = 0
Thread[#31,ForkJoinPool-1-worker-1,5,CarrierThreads]
    org.example.DemoPinnedThread.causesPinning
    (DemoPinnedThread.java:24) <== monitors:1
```

It contains less information than the full description. From practical experience, we can say that the full description is nicer to work with if the pinning is caused in third-party libraries. The short description really shines when you work with the threads directly like in the previous example.

When you need to debug where the virtual thread is pinned, you should use the full description. This gives you a lot more information to work with. The full description is especially useful when the pinning happens in third-party libraries.

When Not to Use Virtual Threads

Virtual threads are a great new feature for the Java language but are not a silver bullet. They don't perform optimally in every situation. This is because of how they are implemented and work behind the scenes. Let's go over some scenarios you should try to avoid when working with virtual threads.

The first one would be to pool virtual threads. You should never pool virtual threads; they are made to be cheap to create. One of the creators of virtual threads says that when you are in a situation where you pool virtual threads, you must rethink your design. With Java 21, you can let go of threads having to be an expensive resource.

Also, don't use a pool to limit access to a resource. There are some cases where developers choose to use a pool to limit, for example, the number of connections to a database. So, with virtual threads, you may be tempted to do something like the following:

```
ThreadFactory factory = Thread.ofVirtual().factory();

try(ExecutorService vte = Executors.newFixedThreadPool(5,
factory)){
        // make call to an external resource
}
```

This would limit the connections to only five. While this may work, it is not an ideal situation. To improve this code example, use a semaphore instead. Look at the following example to see how this improves the code:

```
public static void main(String[] args) {

    Semaphore s = new Semaphore(10);

    Runnable task = () -> {
        try {
            s.acquire();

            // make call to external resource
        } catch (InterruptedException e) {
            throw new RuntimeException(e);
        } finally {
            s.release();
        }
    };
```

```
try(ExecutorService vte = Executors.
newVirtualThreadPerTaskExecutor()){
    for (int i = 0; i < 1000; i++) {
        vte.submit(task);
    }
}

}
```

With the semaphore, you can switch to a thread per task model. You only need to create tasks/virtual threads. The lock will make sure only a limited number of threads access the resource at the same time.

Another important thing to keep in mind when wanting to use virtual threads is how often they are going to block and for how long. This is important to know and compare them to using platform threads. If a virtual thread never blocks or only once for a very short period, it could be better to use platform threads instead.

Another less obvious case is when your virtual threads block often but only for a very short time. This causes the virtual threads to be unmounted and mounted every blocking method. While this happens very fast, it's not for free. The important thing is to measure the performance of the application using tools like Java Microbenchmark Harness.

Summary

In this chapter, you learned how concurrency worked in Java prior to version 21. You learned what virtual threads are and these threads run on carrier threads. These carrier threads do the hard work of running the tasks. These carrier threads switch to a new virtual thread every time a thread is blocked. We talk about tasks because with virtual threads you can switch to a thread per task model. You also learned that not every workload performs better on virtual threads. When you use these new threads, you need to think about how often they block and for how long. Otherwise, platform threads would outperform them.

CHAPTER 2

Structured Concurrency

Structured concurrency was the second delivery from Project Loom, right after the virtual threads we introduced in Chapter 1. In this chapter, we will

- Look at what structured concurrency is
- Look at an example using structured concurrency
- Dive into the underlying API with StructuredTaskScope
- Create a custom StructuredTaskScope implementation
- Look at some alternatives to structured concurrency

What Is Structured Concurrency?

Structured concurrency lets you reason about concurrent code by using well-defined points where the execution is branched into multiple tasks and where these results are joined again. It is to concurrency what for loops and i-branches are to structured programming. It allows you to limit the lifetime of a concurrent operation to a specific scope. In structured programming, if we have an if statement, the lifetime of variables defined within the body of the if block is constrained to that block. They cannot leak outside the if block. The same is true for structured concurrency:

© Ron Veen and David Vlijmincx 2024
R. Veen and D. Vlijmincx, *Virtual Threads, Structured Concurrency, and Scoped Values*,
Apress Pocket Guides, https://doi.org/10.1007/979-8-8688-0500-4_2

outside of the scope, the operations do not exist, ensuring that no threads of execution are on the loose, thus preventing them from creating memory leaks or consuming unnecessary CPU resources.

To fully understand the power and ease of use of structured concurrency, we should look at what its counterpart is. What is unstructured concurrency?

Unstructured Concurrency

Let us start with looking at what unstructured concurrency in Java entails. Look at the following code example. It uses the Weather API. In the code, we try to retrieve both the current weather for New York as well as the forecast and historical data. We are doing so by submitting three individual requests to an ExecutorService.

```
try (ExecutorService es = Executors.
newVirtualThreadPerTaskExecutor()) {
    var currentFuture  = es.submit(this::getCurrent);
    var forecastFuture = es.submit(this::getForecast);
    var historyFuture  = es.submit(this::getHistory);

    return new Result(currentFuture.get(),
                            forecastFuture.get(),
                            historyFuture.get());
```

Now what if one of these requests fails? We probably cannot satisfy the request from our user as we will not have all required data available. But we have no means of terminating the two remaining requests, even though we will never use the output.

Similarly, if the user decides to cancel their request, we have no possibility of cancelling the three tasks we submitted to the ExecutorService.

Things become even more complicated based on what thread is started first and who throws the exception, but thread leakage will occur.

Tasks that are executed via an `ExecutorService` are typically deemed as unstructured tasks. They are invoked individually, and they have no direct relation to other tasks that are started by that same `ExecutorService`.

Structured Concurrency

Now that we have an idea what unstructured concurrency is, let us see how structured concurrency can improve on it. The idea is that we have a task that can consist of subtasks, which themselves can contain subtasks again. So, in fact, we have a tree-like structure of tasks that require execution. The lifetime of this structure is bound to the lifetime of the block in which it is defined. Within the Java structured concurrency API, this is called `StructuredTaskScope`, but more on that in the next section. When this scope is closed, it is guaranteed that all tasks and subtasks have either been completed or cancelled.

StructuredTaskScope

The `StructuredTaskScope<T>` is the main class of the structured concurrency API which is located in the java.util.concurrent package. It is a small API in that it consists of only six public methods and two protected methods. These methods are

```
public <U extends T> Subtask<U> fork(Callable<? extends
U> task);
public StructuredTaskScope<T> join( );
public StructuredTaskScope<T> joinUntil(Instant deadline);
public void close( );
public void shutdown( );
```

```
public boolean isShutdown( );
protected void ensureOwnerAndJoined);
protected void handleComplete(StructuredTaskScope.SubTask <?
extends T> subTask);
```

Basic Example of StructuredTaskScope

Let us have a look at a basic example of how to use StructuredTaskScope. It is for explanation purposes only. You are more likely to use some direct subclasses of StructuredTaskScope, which have a different implementation of the handleComplete method. Or you could even write your own subclass of StructuredTaskScope, as we will see later in this chapter. Writing your own subclasses is generally not needed, but if you find that the supplied implementations do not meet your requirements, you have the freedom to create your own.

Here is the example:

```
try (var scope = new StructuredTaskScope<String>()) {

            Supplier<String> currentSubtask = scope.
            fork(this::getCurrent);
            Supplier<String> forecastSubtask = scope.
            fork(this::getForecast);
            Supplier<String> historySubtask = scope.
            fork(this::getHistory);

            scope.join();

            return new Result(currentSubtask.get(),
                             forecastSubtask.get(),
                             historySubtask.get());

    }

Schematically, it looks like this:
```

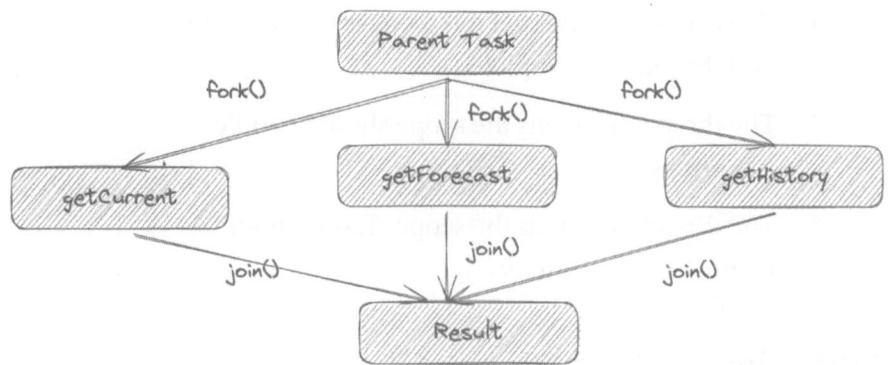

Figure 2-1. *Schematic representation of our StructuredTaskScope*

Let us dissect what is happening here. First, we create a new
StructuredTaskScope within a try-with-resources block. This is
important because StructuredTaskScope implements the AutoCloseable
interface. This interface will guarantee that the close method of the
StructuredTaskScope will be called by the runtime once we have finished
the try-with-resources block.

Next, we specify the three tasks that we want to have executed
concurrently by passing the methods to execute to the fork method. Note
that the fork method returns a SubTask object. It is recommended to cast
it to a Supplier though. This is because SubTask extends the Supplier
interface.

Finally, we call join. This will make the current thread wait for all tasks
in the scope to be completed or for the scope to be shut down.

Once all tasks are completed, our thread continues, and we can invoke
get() on the subtasks to retrieve the results.

From this, we can see the general flow for structured concurrency:

1. Create the task scope, the root for all subtasks.

2. Create any number of subtasks in this scope.

3. The thread that created the scope is joining the
    scope (and all subtasks implicitly).

4. The thread that created the scope is blocking until all subtasks are completed.

5. The thread that owns the scope should handle any errors.

6. The thread that owns the scope closes it upon completion (automatically).

Subtasks

We should talk a little more about the Subtask<T> interface that is returned from the join method. It is located in the java.util.concurrent package as well.

At first glance, the join method seems to return a Supplier<T>, which in fact is true. But this is only because Subtask implements the Supplier<T> functional interface. The language designers prefer the result of a join operation to be casted to a Supplier instead of a SubTask.

Subtask itself is an interface, or, more precisely, it is a sealed interface. Sealed interfaces allow more fine-grained detail over which classes are permitted to implement them. In the case of Subtask, it permits only one class to implement it, SubtaskImpl.

```
public sealed interface Subtask<T> extends Supplier<T> permits
SubtaskImpl
```

One could say, if there is only one subclass allowed, the interface might just as well have been implemented as a final class. But by using an interface, they have kept the option open to permit further classes to implement the interface in the future. In such a case, only the permit clause of Subclass needs to be extended with this new class. When using a final class, it would not be possible to allow a second (sub)class without breaking the interface. This is a good example of how to stay open for future extensions without worrying too much about them now.

Subtask holds an enum State that indicates if a result for this subtask is available. It has three possible values:

- UNAVAILABLE: Not completed yet or completed after the task scope was shut down

- SUCCESS: Completed with a result available

- FAILED: Completed with an exception, no result available

If the status of a subtask is SUCCESS, then the result can be retrieved by calling get() on the subtask. Calling get() when the subtask has not yet completed or failed to complete will throw an IllegalStateException.

On the contrary, if the status of a subtask is FAILED, then the exception that was thrown during the execution can be found by calling the exception() method of the subtask. Calling exception() when the subtask did not complete yet or completed with a result, will throw an IllegalStateException as well.

SubtaskImpl is, as we saw before, the only class that is allowed to implement the Subtask interface. It is defined like this:

```
private static final class SubtaskImpl<T> implements
Subtask<T>, Runnable
```

We can see that it implements the Runnable interface. When the fork() method of the StructuredTaskContext is called, it is supplied with a Callable. The fork method then creates an instance of SubtaskImpl passing it the callable. The run() method of Runnable that is implemented by SubtaskImpl invokes the call() method on the callable to execute it and retrieve its result. It also registers if an exception was thrown, and if so, it keeps track of this exception, so it can be retrieved at a later time.

Using Virtual Threads by Default

Tasks in structured concurrency are backed by virtual threads by default. In the previous chapter, you have learned the many benefits that virtual threads have over their predecessors, the platform threads.

As such, it should come as no surprise that virtual threads are the default. The default constructor for StructuredTaskContext looks like the following:

```
public StructuredTaskScope() {
        this(null, Thread.ofVirtual().factory());
}
```

Nothing stops you from using platform threads though; you just need to invoke a different constructor. StructuredTaskContext offers this alternative constructor:

```
public StructuredTaskScope(String name, ThreadFactory factory)
```

You can invoke this constructor to start using platform threads instead of virtual threads by supplying the platform thread factory:

```
public StructuredTaskScope() {
        this(null, Thread.ofPlatform().factory());
}
```

Though it is possible to use platform threads, we do strongly advice against it unless you have a compelling reason to do so.

Handling Timeouts

So far, we have seen the join method that tries to complete a task no matter how long it takes to complete. Often, you want to set a limit on how long you are willing to wait for an answer. In such situation, the joinUntil method can be used. Simply supply the maximum wait time as an Instant:

```
public StructuredTaskScope<T> joinUntil(Instant deadline)
        throws InterruptedException, TimeoutException
```

Structured ConcurrencyPolicies

As mentioned, StructuredTaskScope is not intended to be used directly. StructuredTaskScope supplies two subclasses that implement two concurrency design patterns. These patterns, Invoke All and Invoke Any, are not new. They are well-known patterns. In fact, they already existed in the ExecutorService interface that was introduced in Java 8 back in 2014. The methods accepted a collection of callables. But depending on the type of ExecutorService and the type and capacity of the thread pool that backed the actual implementation of the ExecutorService, the behavior could vary. With structured concurrency, the behavior and scope of the tasks are well defined.

The Invoke All Pattern

The Invoke All pattern is the most common pattern of the two default supplied patterns. It allows for spawning multiple subtasks and then waiting until they have all completed successfully or until an exception is thrown by one of the subtasks.

This pattern is implemented by the ShutDownOnFailure static inner class of StructuredTaskScope.

If an exception is thrown by one of the subtasks, it is deemed that no good result can be supplied to the caller, and the entire scope closes down – hence the name, ShutdownOnFailure.

The example we used earlier in this can be rewritten to leverage the ShutdownOnFailure policy in the following way:

```
try (var scope = new StructuredTaskScope.
ShutdownOnFailure()) {                                          // 1

        Supplier<CurrentWeather> currentSubtask = scope.
        fork(this::getCurrent);                          // 2
        Supplier<Forecast> forecastSubtask = scope.
        fork(this::getForecast);
        Supplier<History> historySubtask = scope.
        fork(this::getHistory);

        scope.join();                                    // 3
        scope.throwIfFailed();                           // 4

        return new Result(currentSubtask.get(),          // 5
                        forecastSubtask.get(),
                        historySubtask.get());
    }
```

Let us walk through the preceding code:

1. We create a StructuredTaskScope of type ShutdownOnFailure.

2. We fork three of subtasks.

3. We call scope.join to make the thread that owns the scope wait until all subtasks are completed (and/or exception is thrown).

4. Once the thread owning the scope continues, meaning all subtasks are completed or cancelled, we check if an exception was thrown via scopeIfFailed.

5. After this point, we can safely call get() on the subtasks as we can be assured now that no exception was thrown.

Notice how we define the scope as StructuredTaskScope.Shutdown OnFailure. As said, ShutdownOnFailure is a static final class defined within StructuredTaskScope and extending it.

It uses much of the functionality of StructuredTaskScope, but overrides the protected handleComplete(Subtask) method to add specialized behavior that differs between ShutdownOnSuccess and ShutdownOnFailure.

The actual code for the ShutdownOnFailure.handleComplete method looks like this:

```
@Override
  protected void handleComplete(Subtask<?> subtask) {
      if (subtask.state() == Subtask.State.FAILED
          && firstException == null
          && FIRST_EXCEPTION.compareAndSet(this, null, subtask.
          exception())) {
              super.shutdown();
      }
}
```

As soon as the first subtask finishes with a status Failed, the shutdown() is called on StructuredTaskScope. This will trigger the context to cancel all subtasks that are still executing. The context waits until all subtasks are cancelled and then will shut down itself. No manual intervention from you is required to cancel all remaining tasks. That is just lovely!

This pattern is typically used if we need to retrieve multiple sets of data related to one another. Imagine a customer detail screen that contains the customer's address, a list of their outstanding orders, a list of their most recent completed orders, their outstanding balance, and a list of outstanding returns.

Instead of retrieving this information sequentially, we can retrieve it concurrently while still waiting for all information to be retrieved before continuing. Structured concurrency provides a very easy-to-follow, sequential flow of code that is easy to read, understand, and reason about.

The Invoke Any Pattern

The Invoke Any pattern is kind of the opposite compared to the Invoke All pattern. It is a race: the task that returns a value first wins. The idea is that multiple tasks are started simultaneously. As soon as any of these tasks returns a result, the other tasks that are still executing will be cancelled. If the first result is an exception, all other tasks will be cancelled as well, and the result of the execution will be this exception.

See the following code sample:

```
try (var scope = new StructuredTaskScope.ShutdownOnSuccess<>()) {    // 1

        scope.fork(this::getWeatherData);                               // 2
        scope.fork(this::getOpenWeatherData);

        scope.join();                                                   // 3

        return scope.result();                                          // 4

    }
}
```

In this example, we are retrieving weather data from two different APIs. We do not care to retrieve the data from one specific API, but rather from the API that responds the quickest. This could mean that on every invocation of this method, data from a different API is returned. The importance here is speed and not so much the data itself.

You could imagine a similar situation when retrieving navigational instructions for driving from point A to point B. You could ask multiple providers, for example, Google Maps and Apple Maps, for directions and choose to use the one that responds the quickest.

Let us again step through this code:

1. We create a `StructuredTaskScope` of type `ShutdownOnSuccess`.

2. We fork the subtasks. Note that we do not need to hold a reference to the results of the operation.

3. The scope joins and waits for the first result to be returned.

4. We return the result.

This example looks very similar to the previous one. There are three differences. The first difference is that a different type of `StructuredTaskScope` is created. Second, when forking the subtasks, we do not need to hold a reference to their return values. This is because at most one result will become available, and the API will take care of holding on that result, so we do not have to ask every subtask if it has a result ourselves. And finally, because the `StructuredTaskScope` holds on the result for us, we can simply call `scope.result()` to retrieve the result. If no result is available because none of the subtasks completed successfully, then by default an `ExecutionException` will be thrown. This behavior can be adjusted by overriding the overloaded `result()` function:

```
public <X extends Throwable> T result(Function<Throwable, ?
extends X> esf) throws X
```

Here, the first parameter is a `Supplier` function that returns the desired exception.

As soon as one of the subtasks returns a result, all the other subtasks will be shut down by the `StructuredTaskContext`. You do not need to worry about the cancellations. It will all be taken care of for you. How convenient!

Implementing Our Own Strategy

Imagine we are planning to go on a ski trip. We would like to be sure that there is actually snow in the area we want to visit. We can create a custom task scope that will take a number of possible cities we would consider and ask the Weather API if there is currently any snow.

Our custom SnowPolicy will look like this:

```
public class SnowScope<T> extends StructuredTaskScope<T> {
    private  List<T> results = Collections.synchronizedList
    (new ArrayList<>());

    @Override
    protected void handleComplete(Subtask<? extends T>
    subtask) {
        if (subtask.state() == Subtask.State.SUCCESS) {
            T result = subtask.get();
            results.add(result);
        }
    }

    public List<T> results() {
        return this.results;
    }
}
```

Only tasks that result in a successful return will be considered in the value that is returned from our scope.

This scope can be used in the following way:

```java
public class CustomPolicyExample {

    private static final String API_KEY = "YOUR API KEY";

    public static void main(String... args) throws Exception {
        if (args.length == 0) {
            System.out.println("Usage: java CustomPolicyExample
            <space-seperated list of cities>");
            System.exit(0);
        }
        new CustomPolicyExample().run(List.of(args));
    }

    private void run(List<String> cities) throws Exception{
        try(var scope = new SnowScope<CityWeather>()) {
            for (var city : cities) {
                scope.fork(() -> getWeather (city));
            }
            scope.join();
            scope.results().stream()
                .filter(e -> e.current().condition().
                text().contains("snow"))
                .collect(Collectors.toList())
                .forEach(System.out::println);
        }

    }
```

```
private CityWeather getWeather(String city) throws
Exception {
    var uri = StringTemplate.STR."http://api.weatherapi.
    com/v1/current.json?key=\{API_KEY}&q=\{city}";

    var request = HttpRequest.newBuilder()
            .uri(new URI(uri))
            .GET()
            .build();
    try(var client = HttpClient.newHttpClient()) {
        var response = client.send(request, HttpResponse.
        BodyHandlers.ofString());
        CityWeather cw = new Gson().fromJson(response.
        body(), CityWeather.class);
        return cw;
    }
}
}
}
```

The main method receives a number of cities that we would consider from the command line. It then creates an instance of our class and passes each of the parameters to the run method.

The run method will create our custom scope and will for each city call the fork method on the scope, passing on the city. The fork method calls the getWeather method for the city. It will then call join to wait for all tasks to complete. Once completed, it will retrieve the results and filter them on a condition containing the term "snow."

The getWeather method uses the HttpClient to retrieve the current weather data for the given city by calling the Weather API.

The sample code can be found in the github folder along with batch files for compiling and running the sample application. Note that we are using the Gson library to parse the JSON that is returned by the API. You should set your own API key in the API_KEY field of the sample application.

Structured Concurrency Alternatives

Structured concurrency is not a new concept, and Java already has some alternative concurrency implementations. In fact, in JEP-428 (Java Enhancement Proposal) that initially described structured concurrency, it was stated that its goal was "not to replace any of the concurrency constructs in java.util.concurrent". Neither was its goal "to define the definitive structured concurrency API for Java."

There are some alternatives already available, and we will look at two of these. There are the Completable Futures, which are part of the standard JDK, and there is the reactive programming solution, implemented by third-party libraries.

Completable Futures

Completable Futures were added to Java in version 8. They provide an asynchronous implementation of the Future interface. They allow for advanced chaining of operations. It is built around the concept of a CompletionStage. This is a, potentially asynchronous, computation that is performed. A stage can be triggered by the completion of a different stage or even stages.

Here is a simple example:

```
private void run() throws Exception{
    CompletableFuture<String> hello = CompletableFuture.
    supplyAsync(() -> "Hello");
    CompletableFuture<String> world = CompletableFuture.
    supplyAsync(() -> "World!");

    CompletableFuture<String> result = hello.thenCombine
    (world, (a, b) -> a + "," + b);
    System.out.println(result.get());
}
```

We define two CompletionStage suppliers that each provide a value. A third CompletionStage is based on the first CompletionStage which is handed the second CompletionStage plus a function that is executed with the values of the two Completion Stages as parameters. On this final CompletionStage, the get() method is called to retrieve the value.

In the initial design of structured concurrency, Futures were used as the return value from a fork operation. This was later changed (while the API was still in preview) to Subtask. It was deemed that CompletableFutures are most useful when they are not completed yet, and their values can be used in ongoing computation. The result of a fork() operation of a structured concurrency task, however, has already received its final resulting values. As such, using CompletableFutures as the outcome of a task has no additional value and is even confusing.

Reactive Programming

Reactive programming is a programming paradigm that has gained much attention in recent years. It is based on the Reactive Manifesto that was created in 2013. In this document, the features of a reactive system are described. These are responsiveness, resilience, elasticity, and message driven.

Reactive programming has several concepts, such as

- Producers
- Consumers
- Processors
- Streams

The basic concept is that reactive programming reacts to events instead of waiting for them to happen, hence the name. It works with asynchronous data in a non-blocking way.

In Java, there are several frameworks that implement or support reactive programming. The best-known ones are

- RxJava

- Project Reactor

- Akka

- Spring Reactive Streams

The following is a very simple example of reactive programming, which contains all the main components:

```
import reactor.core.publisher.Flux;
import reactor.core.scheduler.Schedulers;

public class ReactiveExample {
    public static void main(String[] args)
    {
        Flux<String> flux = Flux.just("R", "e", "a", "c",
        "t", "i", "v", "e");                          // 1

        flux
            .map(s -> s.toUpperCase())                // 2
            .publishOn(Schedulers.parallel())         // 3
            .subscribe(System.out::println);          // 4
        try {
            Thread.sleep(1000);
        }
        catch (InterruptedException e) {
            e.printStackTrace();
        }
    }
}
```

We create a stream of data (1), which is processed (2) before being published (3), while a subscriber (4) listens for the published data.

Reactive programming has a few drawbacks:

- It requires a different mindset and thus has a steeper learning curve.

- It can introduce additional complexity into an application which makes it more difficult to reason about the flow of an application.

- Debugging reactive applications is notoriously difficult due to its asynchronous and concurrent behavior.

Virtual threads paired with structured concurrency aim to address the limitations of concurrent programming in Java and remove the drawbacks of reactive programming by allowing to write code that is easier to write, debug, and understand.

Summary

In this chapter, we have looked at the new structured concurrency API in Java. We have seen what its main components are and how the basic flow is. We have looked at the different policies that are by default available. We have also implemented our own alternative policy. Finally, we looked at potential alternatives to structured concurrency.

CHAPTER 3

Scoped Values

After virtual threads and structured concurrency, scoped values are the third delivery from Project Loom. They are intended to replace the long-serving ThreadLocal variables and work better with virtual threads.

In this chapter, we are going to refresh your memory on what exactly ThreadLocals are and why we need them. Then we will look at why there is a need to replace them. And finally, we are going to have a detailed look at their successors, the scoped values.

What Are ThreadLocal Variables Again?

ThreadLocal variables are variables that are connected to a certain thread. Their value is unique and restricted to a specific thread and can only be accessed from that thread. For instance, Thread-1 and Thread-2 have access to a ThreadLocal variable called *count*. Each of these two threads will have their own unique value for this variable. And each thread can only access its own value, but never the value of the other thread.

From this, it becomes clear that ThreadLocals have a per-thread value that is unique for the executing thread. This makes it sound very much like it is a kind of hidden parameter, which in fact it is.

Imagine a situation where we have a web application in which a user is required to sign in. When the user is updating data, their *user-id* will be added to the modified data to have an audit trail. The user will make a request to a web service. In the web service, the *user-id* is retrieved from a request

© Ron Veen and David Vlijmincx 2024
R. Veen and D. Vlijmincx, *Virtual Threads, Structured Concurrency, and Scoped Values*,
Apress Pocket Guides, https://doi.org/10.1007/979-8-8688-0500-4_3

parameter. But to get to the part of the code that updates the database, it might need to call a chain of business methods in between. Now, all these methods need to have the user-id as a parameter. And when it is decided that an update comment from the user is required as well, we need to add this additional parameter to all these methods. Not only is this cumbersome, but this might also lead to overly long parameter lists, which is a code smell.

In such situations, it might be better, and easier, to use ThreadLocal variables. When a request arrives at the web server, a thread will be assigned to process this request. These threads will usually come from a thread pool. This thread can then create the required ThreadLocals and assign them their values. Each method that is processed from within the thread can access the values unique to that thread.

How ThreadLocals Work

Let us have a look at a simple example of the usage of ThreadLocals. Have a look at the following code:

```java
import java.util.concurrent.atomic.AtomicInteger;

public class SimpleLocalThreads implements Runnable {

    private static final AtomicInteger value = new
    AtomicInteger(100);

    private static final ThreadLocal<Integer> COUNTER = new
    ThreadLocal<>() {
        @Override
        protected Integer initialValue() {
            System.out.println("Getting the next value for a
            new thread ");
            return value.incrementAndGet();
        }
    };
```

```
@Override
public void run() {
    System.out.println(Thread.currentThread().getName() +
    " : " + COUNTER.get());
}

public static void main(String... args) throws
InterruptedException {
    var r = new SimpleLocalThreads();
    for (var i=0; i < 10; i++) {
        Thread.sleep(200);
        Thread.ofVirtual().name("Thread " + i).start(r);
    }
}

}
```

We are creating a class that implements the Runnable interface. This means we must implement the run() method. In it, we simply print the current thread's value for the ThreadLocal Counter variable.

This variable is set when we create a new Thread. We have overridden the initialValue() method of our ThreadLocal and supply the next value from an AtomicInteger. We use an AtomicInteger as it will guard us against race conditions when incrementing the value from multiple threads.

If you run the example, the output will look something like this:

```
Getting the next value for a new thread
Thread 0 : 101
Getting the next value for a new thread
Thread 1 : 102
Getting the next value for a new thread
Thread 2 : 103
```

```
Getting the next value for a new thread
Thread 3 : 104
Getting the next value for a new thread
Thread 4 : 105
```

. . .

The output shows that each time we create a new Thread, initialValue() of the ThreadLocal *COUNTER* is called to retrieve and assign a value specific for this thread to the *COUNTER* variable.

How ThreadLocals Work Internally

You might be wondering, how do ThreadLocals achieve this quite remarkable feat? The answer lies within its implementation.

Every thread has a ThreadLocalMap:

```
ThreadLocal.ThreadLocalMap threadLocals;
```

The ThreadLocalMap is a customized HashMap where the key contains the ThreadLocals hashcode and the value is the thread's value for the ThreadLocal variable.

ThreadLocalMap is a collection of all the ThreadLocal variables that are known for this thread. Remarkably, this map is not maintained by the Thread class itself, but by the ThreadLocal class. Look at what the set() method of ThreadLocal does:

```
private void set(Thread t, T value) {
    ThreadLocalMap map = getMap(t);
    if (map != null) {
        map.set(this, value);
    } else {
        createMap(t, value);
    }
}
```

The method tries to retrieve a `ThreadLocalMap` from the given `Thread`. If a map is found, it adds (or overwrites) the current entry. If no such map is found, a new map is created.

Looking at the `getMap()` method in more detail, this is what it does:

```
ThreadLocalMap getMap(Thread t) {
    return t.threadLocals;
}
```

It returns all `ThreadLocal` variables of the `Thread`.

Advantages of ThreadLocals

Using ThreadLocals has several advantages. Let us look at these in a little more detail.

Thread Safety

`ThreadLocal` variables are inherently thread-safe, and they remove the need to use shared resources. This quality means that you do not need to use synchronization in your code, making it potentially much more performant and much cleaner.

Storing Contextual Information

As we already saw in the introduction, ThreadLocals can be used to store all kinds of contextual information, like user sessions, credentials, transactions, and database connections. Not having to pass these around makes your code cleaner and less vulnerable to change.

Thread-Specific Configuration

ThreadLocals can be used for thread-specific configuration. A common example is storing locale information depending on the current user in a ThreadLocal or a specific logging level. Another well-known use is storing SimpleDateFormat in a ThreadLocal. SimpleDateFormat is not thread-safe, but by having an instance per thread, you can work around this limitation.

Disadvantages of ThreadLocals

With all the advantages mentioned in the previous section, you might wonder why we need a replacement for ThreadLocals. As it turns out, ThreadLocals have some serious disadvantages too. And with the introduction of virtual threads and its nearly limitless scalability, these disadvantages become even more highlighted.

The following sections assume that we have this ThreadLocal variable defined:

```
public static final ThreadLocal<String> API_KEY = new
ThreadLocal<>();
```

Mutable State

Mutable state is one of the problems with ThreadLocals. Although a ThreadLocal might already have a value, this value can be easily changed with the following method:

```
public void set(T value)
```

Our API key defined above can be changed at any point in the code where it is accessible. And being a public static variable, this is in essence **everywhere**. We could update the value like this:

```
API_KEY.set("the_secret_api_key");
```

While this might seem convenient at first glance, it is not. As ThreadLocals are often defined as both public and static, they can be considered global variables. And we all know that global state is troublesome. If any method can change a variable, then how are you going to identify which one did it? If a ThreadLocals value is changed in multiple places, it is much harder to reason about the code. And debugging any errors related to this quickly become a nightmare.

Memory Leaks

The second disadvantage of ThreadLocals is that they can easily create memory leaks. Platform threads are an expensive resource, both in creation time and memory usage. For this reason, they are often pooled in ExecutorServices, so they can be re-used instead of re-created.

This means that once a thread is done executing, it is returned to the thread pool. If any ThreadLocal variables are not cleared at that time, they will live on. Even though the key to the internal HashMap that stores the ThreadLocal variables is a WeakReference type, the thread is still holding a reference to the object, and the ThreadLocal will never become eligible for garbage collection. ThreadLocals can be removed from a thread by calling public void remove( ) on the ThreadLocal. But an analysis of large Java codebases has shown that this is something that is often forgotten.

Our API key ThreadLocal could be cleaned easily by executing this code:

```
API_KEY.remove();
```

This will remove the value from the **current** thread from the ThreadLocal.

An alternative approach would be to overwrite the afterExecute method of the ThreadPoolExecutor class.

ThreadLocals Everywhere

The third problem with ThreadLocals is memory consumption. When a thread spawns child threads, then these child threads will by default get the ThreadLocal variables from the parent thread where there is a value set in the parent thread. This behavior can be overridden, by overriding the `protected T childValue(T parentValue)` method from `InheritableThreadLocal`. But I have never come across code that did so.

As the ThreadLocals have mutable state, it is not sufficient for the Java runtime to simply pass a reference to the object. The value might change between methods. This means that each child thread will get its own copy of the value. Now, this might not be a problem when dealing with platform threads, as we normally would only have a few hundred to a few thousand of them. But when we are using virtual threads, of which we can have a few million within a single machine, this copying of values very quickly becomes a problem. It is not unlikely that the JVM will run out of available memory.

Introducing Scoped Values

Now that we have seen how ThreadLocals work and which problems they can cause, this beckons the question of what the alternative is. The third delivery from Project Loom, after virtual threads and structured concurrency, is scoped values. In this section, we are going to look at what scoped values are, how they can be used, and what problems they solve. And finally, we investigate some methods of the scoped values API.

A Simple ScopedValue Example

Let us start with an example of the usage of scoped values:

```java
public class ScopedValueExample {

    public static final ScopedValue<String> USER =
    ScopedValue.newInstance();                          // 1

    public static void main(String... args) {
        new ScopedValueExample().execute();
    }

    Runnable runnable = () -> {                          // 2
        System.out.println(String.format
        ("Authenticating user %s",                      // 2
            USER.get()));                               // 2
    };

    private void execute() {
        ScopedValue.where(USER, "Duke")                 // 3
                .run(runnable);                         // 4
    }

}
```

There are several interesting facts. In the line marked "**1**," we define a scoped value. Creating it is easy; we can simply call the newInstance( ) static factory method on the ScopedValue class. Note that we do not set an initial value for the scoped variable here.

In the lines marked with "**2**," we define a lambda expression that implements the Runnable interface. Inside, it retrieves the value for the ScopedValue variable we defined earlier. The value can be simply retrieved by invoking the get( ) method on a ScopedValue. You should take some precautions when doing this – more on that a little later in this chapter.

We assign a value to the ScopedValue variable in the line marked "**3**." Note that we use the method where( ) to assign the value. We name the ScopedValue variable and the value we want to assign to it.

Finally, in the line marked with "**4**," we call the run( ) method supplying the Runnable we want to execute.

This is the essence of ScopedValues: the value "Duke" will only be visible to the Runnable that is being executed by the run( ) method and all the methods that are being called from that method.

This is why they are named ScopedValues; the existence and visibility of these variables is scoped to the execution of the Runnable and all the methods invoked directly or indirectly from that Runnable.

In this example, we used the Runnable interface and called the run( ) method on the ScopedValue class. ScopedValues also supports the Callable interface. Instead of calling the run( ) method, you need to use the call( ) method. Here is an example of how that might look:

```
Callable<String> callable = () -> {
    System.out.println(String.format("Authenticating
    user %s", USER.get()));
    return USER.get().toLowerCase();
};

private void execute() throws Exception{
    var value = ScopedValue.where(USER, "Duke")
            .call(callable);
    System.out.println(String.format("Returned value: %s",
    value));
}
```

When we only bind one ScopedValue to a method execution, we can use a shorthand like this:

```
ScopedValue.runWhere(USER, "Duke", runnable);
```

The same is also available for Callables:

```
ScopedValue.callWhere(USER, "Duke", callable);
```

Supplying More Than One ScopedValue

The ScopedValue API is set up with the intention that the number of ScopedValues that are being supplied to a method is limited. This makes sense; the opposite would be a code smell, just as having many ThreadLocal variables is one. But where ThreadLocals have an application-wide scope, ScopedValues are limited to one routine, which would make the code smell even stronger.

Nevertheless, it is possible to supply multiple values to a method. Look at the following modified version of the preceding method:

```
ScopedValue.where(USER, "Duke")
       .where(PWD, "s3cr3t")
       .where(API_KEY, "THE_SECRET_KEY")
       .run(runnable);
```

You can see that passing multiple ScopedValues can be easily done via repeating the where( ) method.

Running the code will provide this output:

```
java --enable-preview --source 21 ScopedValueExample.java
Password: s3cr3t
Api Key : THE_SECRET_KEY
```

When No Value Is Bound

We have said earlier that using the get( ) method to retrieve a ScopedValue can be dangerous. If it turns out that no value is set for the ScopedValue that the method wants to retrieve, a NoSuchElementException will be thrown – not something you want to happen in your production code.

To prevent such an exception from occurring, you should always check if a value is set. In fact, the official phrase is "check if a value is **bound** for the method." There is a method that can do the checking for you:

```
public boolean isBound()
```

Here is the modified version of our Runnable example from before:

```
Runnable runnable = () -> {
    System.out.println(String.format("Authenticating user
    %s", USER.isBound() ? USER.get() : "Unknown"));
};
```

The code first checks to see if the USER ScopedValue is bound to the context of the method. Remember that in the case of a Runnable, it is the run( ) method that is anonymously implemented by the lambda expression. If the value for USER is bound to the method context, isBound( ) will return true, and the value for the ScopedValue variable can be safely retrieved. If no value is bound, isBound( ) will return false.

There are two other methods that can be used as an alternative to isBound. The first one is

```
public T orElse(T other)
```

Instead of throwing a NoSuchElementException, this method will simply return the value supplied via "*other*." The rewritten version of our example Runnable will become like this:

```
Runnable runnable = () -> {
    System.out.println(String.format("Authenticating
    user %s", USER.orElse("Unknown")));
};
```

The other method allows you to define an alternative Exception being thrown instead of the standard NoSuchElementException. This might prove handy if you would rather throw some customized business-logic exception. The method signature is

```
public <X extends Throwable> T orElseThrow(Supplier<? extends X> exceptionSupplier) throws X
```

As can be seen from the method signature, we can define a Supplier that should return a class that implements the Throwable interface. Throwable of course is the base class of all errors and exceptions, both checked and unchecked, in Java.

The modified Runnable looks like this:

```
Runnable runnable = () -> {
    System.out.println(String.format("Authenticating user
    %s", USER.orElseThrow(IllegalArgumentException::new)));
};
```

Summing Up Scoped Values

Before we investigate some other details of ScopedValues, we think this is a good time to summarize the ways in which ScopedValues tries to solve the limitations and problems of ThreadLocals.

We recognized mutable state as one of the problems. This is addressed by ScopedValues in a simple and precise manner: the value is set via one or more where( ) methods before invoking the method. Once set, the value cannot be changed anymore; it is immutable. There is the possibility to rebind a ScopedValue for a method, but more on that a little later.

The second problem of ThreadLocals was memory leakage. No such thing with ScopedValues. The values are bound before a method is executed, and afterward it is guaranteed that the values will be unbound again. It makes no difference if the method completes successfully or with an exception, the values will always be unbound after the method execution is complete. This is done automatically. So, memory will always be cleaned, and no memory leakage should occur from using ScopedValues.

The immutability of ScopedValue also helps in circumventing the third problem of ThreadLocals: copying values all around. When values do not change, there is no need to make a copy of a value and pass it to a child method. Immutable values can be passed by reference. Having the ability to pass a reference, which is basically a pointer, is way cheaper in terms of memory consumption, and performance, than passing the original value.

Scope Binding Revisited

We would like to return one more time to the concept of binding ScopedValues to a method context. We will look at an example where a ScopedValue is bound and one where it is not. And we will also look at how a method that has a ScopedValue can supply a different value for the same ScopedValue for a method it calls itself. This process is called rebinding.

Standard Binding

Let us have a look at the following code to explain in detail how binding works:

```
public class ScopedValueBoundExample {
    public static final ScopedValue<String> USER = ScopedValue.
    newInstance();
    public static void main(String... args) {
        new ScopedValueBoundExample().execute();
    }
}
```

```java
Runnable runnable = () -> {
    System.out.println("Inside runnable: USER bound="
    + USER.isBound()
            + " => " + USER.get());              // 3
    otherMethod();                               // 4
};

private void otherMethod() {
    System.out.println("Inside otherMethod:
    USER bound=" + USER.isBound() + " => " +
    USER.get());                                 // 5
}

private void execute() {
    System.out.println("Before: USER bound=" + USER.
    isBound());                                  // 1
    ScopedValue.where(USER, "Duke").run(runnable);  // 2
    System.out.println("After: USER bound=" + USER.
    isBound());                                  // 6
    }

}
```

At "**1**," we try to see if the *USER* ScopedValue is bound to the current executing routine, the execute method. As it is not, the print statement will print *"false".* At "**2**," we bind the ScopedValue *USER* by assigning it a value and then call the Runnable. In the Runnable, at "**3**," we check if *USER* is bound to this method. As it is, it prints *"true"* and the value *"Duke."*

We then call "**4**" from this method, with a bounded ScopedValue, another method, called otherMethod. In otherMethod, we then check to see if *USER* is also bound to this routine. As otherMethod is called from a method that has the *USER* ScopedValue bound to its context, this variable is also bound to otherMethod. Thus, the check for isBound() in otherMethod, at "**5**," returns *true*, and again *"Duke"* is printed.

Finally, the Runnable is completed, and we return to the execute( ) method; we check if *USER* is still bound now that the method invocation is complete. As ScopedValues are automatically unbound after the method execution, isBound( ) will return *false*.

Running this program will produce the following output:

```
% java --enable-preview --source 21 ScopedValueBoundExample.java
Before: USER bound=false
Inside runnable: USER bound=true => Duke
Inside otherMethod: USER bound=true => Duke
After: USER bound=false
```

Rebinding a ScopedValue

What if, in the previous example, you wanted to supply a different value for *USER* to otherMethod? This can simply be achieved by providing a new value for the *USER* ScopedValue in the Runnable. Have a look at the updated method:

```
Runnable runnable = () -> {
    System.out.println("Inside runnable: USER bound=" +
    USER.isBound() + " => " + USER.get());
    ScopedValue.where(USER, "Duchess").run
    (this::otherMethod);                             };
```

We print the current value of *USER* and rebind it to the value *"Duchess"* before we call otherMethod. We enter the runnable; the value of USER will be "Duke." During execution of otherMethod, its value will be *"Duchess."* Upon completion of otherMethod, the *USER* ScopedValue will have its original value, *"Duke,"* restored. This is the concept of nested scopes.

The output will look like this:

```
% java --enable-preview --source 21
RebindScopedValueBoundExample.java
Before: USER bound=false
Inside runnable: USER bound=true => Duke
Inside otherMethod: USER bound=true => Duchess
After: USER bound=false
```

Final Thoughts

We hope that you can see the many benefits that ScopedValue has over ThreadLocal variables and that you might consider using them in your next project. At the time of writing this book, ScopedValues are still a preview feature, meaning that they have not become part of the Java standard language yet. It is our expectation, however, that this will happen in Java 23, to be released in September 2024. Nothing much has changed in the ScopedValues API since the previous preview.

In fact, structured concurrency is also still in preview and is likely to become a standard part of Java in version 23 as well, even more so because structured concurrency uses ScopedValues as the default mechanism since its second preview.

But you should not worry for your existing code and frameworks that still use ThreadLocals. They are not going to disappear from the Java language anytime soon. There is simply too much code out there that still relies on them.

Summary

We have introduced ThreadLocals and why you would want to use them. We also saw their advantages and disadvantages. Then we introduced ScopedValues and how elegantly they solve the problems that may arise from the use of ThreadLocals, especially when combined with virtual threads.

This concludes the introduction of the three main deliveries of Project Loom.

CHAPTER 4

Concurrency Patterns

Virtual threads are, as you have learned throughout this book, a completely different type of threads than we had before in Java. They come with their own benefits and drawbacks. In this chapter, we will show you a way to reason about these threads. We start off with reasoning about virtual threads as tasks. Later, we will show you how to use these threads in your own Spring and Quarkus applications. We finish this chapter by implementing some common algorithms with virtual threads to give you an idea of how to do so yourself.

How to Reason About Virtual Threads

As you know by now, you can create millions of threads on something as powerful as a laptop. This is a huge deal but also comes with a lot of new challenges, because with a million threads you get a million lifetimes, resources, and contexts you need to manage. That is why we want to show you another way to think about threads, the thread-per-task model. As the name suggests, you create a thread for each task that you have.

A task is a single unit of work. Inside that unit, it has everything it needs to perform the operations it needs to do. So, what should be a task? Ideally, a task would be something that does not depend on other tasks and can be done in parallel, for example, a web server handling incoming requests. Each request could be an independent task that gets to run in its own thread. The benefits of structuring your workload as tasks are as follows:

© Ron Veen and David Vlijmincx 2024
R. Veen and D. Vlijmincx, *Virtual Threads, Structured Concurrency, and Scoped Values*, Apress Pocket Guides, https://doi.org/10.1007/979-8-8688-0500-4_4

- Tasks are clearly defined.

- Tasks have clear boundaries and so does your code.

- Error recovery can be clearly defined in the task.

The thread-per-task model was not recommended in the past because of the resources it used. Virtual threads and scoped values really made resource consumption a lot better, making it possible to use this model.

How to Use Virtual Threads in Your Application

There is a big chance that you already have an application you are building or maintaining, and you want to try out virtual threads. In this section, we will show you how to start using virtual threads with your application code, enable it for Spring, and handle requests in Quarkus with virtual threads.

When switching from one kind of thread to another it is smart to measure the performance of the application before making the change. The performance metrics help you understand where in your codebase it makes the most sense to make changes and where they have the most impact. When measuring the performance of the application, take note of how many CPU and memory are utilized, how many requests the application can handle, and what the response times are. These metrics will give you an insight into how the application is functioning and if switching to virtual threads is worth it.

Before making the switch, please look again at the graph from Chapter 1 that shows the memory usage between virtual and platform threads. If your application is not going to create 1000 or more threads, it may not be worth it to make the switch to this new kind of thread.

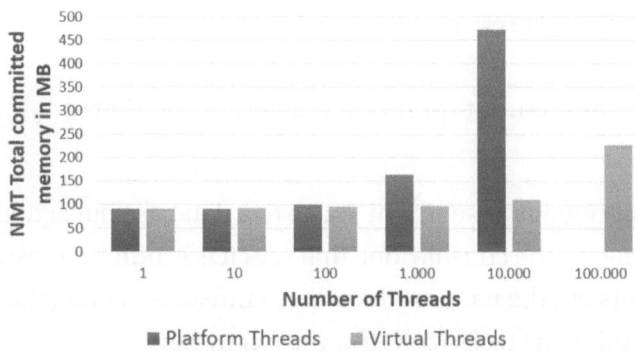

Figure 4-1. *Total memory usage of virtual and platform threads*

The easiest way to make the switch to this new kind of thread is to replace existing executor services with the new virtual thread per task executor. This can be a drop-in replacement, and the application can immediately start using virtual threads. This can cause some problems if the executor service is used as a lock. There are cases where the executor service is used to, for example, limit the number of connections to a database, by using a small pool of threads to perform the database operations. This is not something you can do with virtual threads as you are supposed to create a lot of them. To resolve this issue, you can replace these executors that use a small pool of threads with a virtual thread executor and a semaphore.

Let's make this change a bit more visible with an example. Let's say that we have an application that has a task to send a message to a database. The application uses a pool of threads to limit the number of connections to five. The task is a runnable and looks like the following code example:

```
Runnable sendToDatabase = () -> {
        System.out.println("Send message to a
        database...");
        try {
            Thread.sleep(Duration.ofSeconds(1));
        } catch (InterruptedException e) {
```

```
            throw new RuntimeException(e);
    }
    System.out.println(Thread.currentThread());
};
```

The task pretends to send a message to a database but actually just prints two lines to the console: one that says it is sending a message and one that prints out the name of the current thread executing the task. The executor running the tasks looks like the following:

```
try(var exec = Executors.newFixedThreadPool(5)){
        for (int i = 0; i < 10; i++) {
            exec.submit(sendToDatabase);
        }
    }
```

The executor has a fixed thread pool of five threads. This means that at any moment in time, there are only five threads running a task. Inside the try-with-resource statement is a for loop that submits ten tasks to the executor. The output of this sample code is as follows:

```
Send message to a database...
Send message to a database...
Send message to a database...
Send message to a database...
Send message to a database...
Thread[#33,pool-1-thread-4,5,main]
Thread[#30,pool-1-thread-1,5,main]
Thread[#32,pool-1-thread-3,5,main]
Thread[#34,pool-1-thread-5,5,main]
Thread[#31,pool-1-thread-2,5,main]
```

Only five tasks are active at a given time and print something to the console before the next five tasks are executed. This code works fine, and only five threads are running at the same time. This is fine for platform threads, but with virtual threads we want to create a lot of them to really see their benefits. To limit the number of virtual threads sending a message to the database, we are going to use a semaphore.

You create a semaphore in Java like this:

```
Semaphore s = new Semaphore(5);
```

This creates a semaphore that can give away five permits at a given time. The virtual thread will first have to aquire a permit. If the semaphore as permits left, it will give it to the virtual thread. When the thread is done, it can release the permit so another thread can aquire it. To use a semaphore, we need to change the task a bit. We changed it from a runnable into a method like this:

```
static void sendMessageToDatabase(Semaphore s) {
    try {
        s.acquire();
        System.out.println("Send message to a
        database...");
        Thread.sleep(Duration.ofSeconds(1));
    } catch (InterruptedException e) {
        throw new RuntimeException(e);
    }finally {
        s.release();
    }
    System.out.println(Thread.currentThread());
}
```

The method accepts a semaphore which is used inside the try to aquire a permit. Inside the finally of the try statement is the release of the permit. It's placed there so we are sure that the permit is always released. Changes to the executor service were minimal as you can see:

```
try (var exec = Executors.newVirtualThreadPerTaskExecutor()) {
            Semaphore s = new Semaphore(5);
            for (int i = 0; i < 10; i++) {
                exec.submit(() -> sendMessageToDatabase(s));
            }
        }
```

The only difference is that now a semaphore is created and passed to the method as a parameter. The output of the service also did not change much, as you can see in the following code snippet:

```
Send message to a database...
Send message to a database...
Send message to a database...
Send message to a database...
Send message to a database...
VirtualThread[#32]/runnable@ForkJoinPool-1-worker-8
Send message to a database...
VirtualThread[#34]/runnable@ForkJoinPool-1-worker-1
Send message to a database...
VirtualThread[#36]/runnable@ForkJoinPool-1-worker-3
Send message to a database...
VirtualThread[#33]/runnable@ForkJoinPool-1-worker-3
VirtualThread[#30]/runnable@ForkJoinPool-1-worker-9
....
```

The result of the code is the same, but now it uses virtual threads, and the creation of threads is no longer limited by the pool of threads. Developing your code in this way enables you to create lots of virtual threads but still limit the number of connections to, for example, a database.

Virtual Threads for Web Applications

If you are creating web applications, there is a big chance that you are using Spring or Quarkus. These are two well-known frameworks and offer support for virtual threads. Creating virtual threads yourself inside the application is great, but it is also nice if the framework can handle requests using virtual threads. Let's start with how this is done in Spring Boot and later in this chapter with Quarkus.

For the Spring application, we created a small REST controller that will return hello world. When making a request, it will also print the name of the thread to the console to show what kind of thread is used.

```
@RestController
@RequestMapping(value = "/v1/hello/")
public class HelloWorldController {

    @GetMapping("world")
    String helloWorld(){
        System.out.println(Thread.currentThread());
        return "hello, world!";
    }
}
```

When calling this endpoint, you see the console output like this:

```
Thread[#52,http-nio-8080-exec-1,5,main]
Thread[#54,http-nio-8080-exec-3,5,main]
Thread[#56,http-nio-8080-exec-5,5,main]
Thread[#57,http-nio-8080-exec-6,5,main]
```

By default, Spring will use platform threads to handle requests. To change that, we need to create a property file in the resource directory src/main/resources. Inside the resource directory, create a file named application.properties. Inside the properties file, add this line:

```
spring.threads.virtual.enabled=true
```

71

When you restart the Spring application, it will use virtual threads instead of platform threads to handle requests. The output you will see in the console will reflect the changes:

```
VirtualThread[#62,tomcat-handler-0]/runnable@
ForkJoinPool-1-worker-1
VirtualThread[#69,tomcat-handler-1]/runnable@
ForkJoinPool-1-worker-1
VirtualThread[#70,tomcat-handler-2]/runnable@
ForkJoinPool-1-worker-1
VirtualThread[#71,tomcat-handler-3]/runnable@
ForkJoinPool-1-worker-1
```

As you can see, the requests are now handled by virtual threads. You now know how to make this chance with Spring. Let's now look at how to do the same with a Quarkus application. The endpoint in the Quarkus application that we want to change looks like the following:

```
@Path("/hello")
public class ExampleResource {

    @GET
    @Produces(MediaType.TEXT_PLAIN)
    public String hello() {
        System.out.println(Thread.currentThread());
        return "Hello from Quarkus";
    }
}
```

Just as with the Spring application, this REST endpoint will return some text and print the name of the thread to the console. By default, it uses platform threads, and the result looks like this:

```
Thread[#134,executor-thread-1,5,main]
Thread[#134,executor-thread-1,5,main]
```

To tell Quarkus that we want to use virtual threads instead of platform threads, we need to use the @RunOnVirtualThread annotation on the method. This annotation tells Quarkus that it should be using virtual threads to handle this request. With the annotation, the method looks like this:

```
@GET
    @Produces(MediaType.TEXT_PLAIN)
    @RunOnVirtualThread
    public String hello() {
        System.out.println(Thread.currentThread());
        return "Hello from Quarkus";
    }
```

And now when you call this method, it will print the name of a virtual thread to the console:

```
VirtualThread[#154,quarkus-virtual-thread-0]/runnable@
ForkJoinPool-1-worker-1
VirtualThread[#161,quarkus-virtual-thread-1]/runnable@
ForkJoinPool-1-worker-1
```

As you can see, the approach of supporting virtual threads is different between the frameworks. With Spring, you handle every request with a virtual thread if you change the default setting in the properties file, while with Quarkus you only enable it for the endpoint with the annotation. This can be great if you are not sure about the fact if every endpoint performs better with virtual threads.

Using CompletableFuture<T> with Virtual Threads

The easiest way to use virtual threads with CompletableFuture is to pass an ExecutorService as a parameter to the supplyAsync or runAsync method. In the following example, in lines 2 and 3 you can see the executorService being created and used for the execution of the CompletableFuture:

```
Supplier<String> supplier = () -> "Hello, World!";
ExecutorService executorService = Executors.
newVirtualThreadPerTaskExecutor();
CompletableFuture<String> completableFuture =
CompletableFuture.supplyAsync(supplier, executorService);

CompletableFuture<Void> lastCompatibleFuture =
completableFuture
.thenAccept(s -> System.out.println("Computer says: " + s));

lastCompatibleFuture.get();
executorService.shutdown();
```

When you run this code, it will print the following result to the console:

```
Computer says: Hello, World!
```

While it works, it is not a very pretty code or directly clear to the reader what is going on. That is why I want to show you two alternative ways that make (in my opinion, better) use of virtual threads.

One way to improve the previous example is to use the newVirtualThreadPerTaskExecutor inside a try-with-resource statement. You can use the future returned by the executor later in your code if you need to return a value from a virtual thread:

```
try(var executor = Executors.
newVirtualThreadPerTaskExecutor()){
    Future<String> stringFuture = executor.submit(() ->
    "Computer says: " + supplier.get());
    System.out.println("stringFuture = " + stringFuture.get());
}
```

Running the previous code example will print `stringFuture = Computer says: Hello, World!` to the console.

If you don't need the return value from the virtual thread, you can rewrite the example into something as small as the following example. It does the same, calling the supplier and printing it to the console.

```
Thread thread = Thread.startVirtualThread(() -> System.out.
println("Computer says: " + supplier.get()));
        thread.join();
```

When you run this code, it will print `Computer says: Hello, World!` to the console. What makes this code great is that it is small and concise and shows you exactly what you want the code to do.

Summary

In this chapter, we looked at how to implement virtual threads inside applications. We showed you a new way of thinking about threads in terms of tasks. We looked at how to replace thread pools that were acting as locks with actual locks and a virtual thread executor. The chapter finished with showing you how to use virtual threads to handle requests in your Quarkus and Spring applications and how to use virtual threads with CompletableFuture.

Index

A, B

Async programming, 6, 7
AutoCloseable interface, 4, 31

C

Call() method, 33
Carrier threads, 16–20, 24
CausesPinning, 21
CompletableFutures, 43, 74, 75
CompletionStage, 43, 44

D

Debugging code, 9

E

ExecutorService, 4–6, 28, 29,
    35, 53, 74

F

First in, first out (FIFO) order, 17
fork method, 31, 33, 42

G, H

get( ) method, 55, 57
getMap() method, 51
getWeather method, 42

I

initialValue() method, 49
Invoke All pattern, 35–38
Invoke Any pattern, 38–40

J, K, L

Java language, 22, 63
Java Native Interface (JNI), 19
joinUntil method, 35

M

Mutable state, 52–53

N

NoSuchElementException,
    57–59

© Ron Veen and David Vlijmincx 2024
R. Veen and D. Vlijmincx, *Virtual Threads, Structured Concurrency, and Scoped Values*,
Apress Pocket Guides, https://doi.org/10.1007/979-8-8688-0500-4

O, P

Operating system (OS), 2, 10, 16
otherMethod, 61, 62

Q

Quarkus application, 65, 66,
    71–73, 75

R

Reactive programming, 44
    components, 45
    concepts, 44
    drawbacks, 46
    implement/support, 45
    solution, 43
run( ) method, 56, 58
runAsync method, 74

S

ScheduledThreadPool, 13, 14
ScopedValue, 55–60
Scoped values, 54, 59
    API, 57
    essence, 56
    execute( ) method, 62
    immutability, 60
    lambda expression, 55
    otherMethod, 61
    usage, 55
    USER ScopedValue, 61
    value, 55
    variable, 56

ShutdownOnFailure, 35–37
ShutdownOnSuccess, 37
SnowPolicy, 40
Spring applications, 65, 71, 72, 75
Structured concurrency, 27, 31, 63
    CPU resources, 28
    design, 44
    Java, 43
    programming, 27
    tasks, 34
StructuredTaskContext,
    33, 34, 40
StructuredTaskScope, 29–31,
    35, 37, 39
Subtask, 32, 33
SubtaskImpl, 32, 33

T

ThreadLocalMap, 50, 51
ThreadLocal variables, 47, 49, 50,
    60, 63, 64
    business methods, 48
    contextual information, 51
    disadvantage
        memory consumptions, 54
        memory leaks, 53
    disadvantages, 52
        mutable state, 52
    parameter, 47
    thread-safe, 51
    thread-specific configuration, 52
    usage, 48
    web application, 47

Thread-per-task model, 65, 66
tructuredTaskContext, 33, 34, 40

U

Unstructured concurrency, 28, 29

V, W, X, Y, Z

Virtual() method, 12
VirtualThreadPerTaskExecutor, 14
Virtual threads, 1, 18, 20, 22–24, 34,
  46, 65, 69, 70, 73, 75
 application, 12
 application code, 66
 blocking method, 18

carrier thread, 16, 19
code of the application, 10
database operations, 67
executor service, 4, 6, 15, 68
Java 21, 1, 9, 14
mechanism, 18
memory, 2, 10, 12
number, 15
OS, 2
parameter, 12
platform, 3, 66
properties, 12
RAM, 2
task executor, 67
tasks, 3, 4, 6, 11, 65
web applications, 71